BLACK C(

HUM(

A collection of jokes and sayings compiled by
Winston Homer and Harold Parsons

Plus

Contributions by 'Clebak', Kate Fletcher, Doug
Southall and Jim William Jones.

and

Extracts from Black Country Stories and Sketches
by John Freeman, originally published in 1930.

A Black Country Society Publication

Impressions: 1980, 1984, 1986, 1988, 1990, 1994, 1996,
2000, 2004, 2008, 2012

ISBN 9780 904015 19 5

Acknowledgement:

The Society expresses its thanks to the contributors.

Cover Design: 'Clebak'

Printed by Russell Press, Nottingham

THE BLACK COUNTRY SOCIETY

This voluntary society was founded in 1967 as a reaction to the trend of the late 1950s and early 1960s to amalgamate everything into large units and in the Midlands to sweep away the area's industrial heritage in the process.

The general aim of the Society was and still is to create interest in the past, present and future of the Black Country, and early on, it campaigned for the establishment of an industrial museum. In 1975 the Black Country Museum was started by Dudley Borough Council on 26 acres of totally derelict land adjoining the grounds of Dudley Castle. This has developed into an award-winning museum which attracts 250,000 visitors annually.

All members of the Black Country Society receive the quarterly magazine *The Blackcountryman*, of which over 180 issues have been published since its founding in 1967. In the whole collection there are over 3000 authoritative articles on all aspects of the Black Country by historians, teachers, researchers, students, subject experts and ordinary folk with an extraordinary story to tell. The whole constitutes a unique resource about the area and is a mine of information for students and researchers who frequently refer to it. Many schools and libraries are subscribers. 2000 copies of the magazine are printed each quarter. It is non-commercial and contributors do not receive payment for their articles.

PO Box 71
Kingswinford
West Midlands
DY6 9YN

www.blackcountrysociety.co.uk

publications@blackcountrysociety.co.uk

Two black country singers discussing their offerings at a club concert in which they were both appearing:

"What 'ave yo' just gid 'em, Joe?"

"Cum Into The Garden, Maud. Why, what's yo'rn, Tum?"

"Oh, I'm gooin' ter gie 'em Alice We'er thee bloody bist."

◇   ◇   ◇

A couple of lads at play and hearing a mother call:

"'ay 'er acallin' we?"

"Nah . . . us doe belung to she."

◇   ◇   ◇

"Dad, 'ow dun yo' spell Russia?

"Ar doe 'no."

"Dad . . . what's the naeme o' the French prime minister?"

"Ar doe 'no."

"Dad, what's the longest river in Europe?"

"Ar doe 'no."

"Dad . . . yo' doe mind me keep aski' yo' questions, dun yer?"

"'Corse I doe, lad. If yo' dow ask yo'll never lern."

◇   ◇   ◇

Stable lad at the station goods yard in the days before mechanisation: "Gaffer . . . I gotta tell yer. I's 'ad three 'osses die on me."

"Three? I cor understand that. One 'oss or even tew. But three! 'Ow th' 'ell did it 'appen?"

"Wull, y' see. I opened me pay packet in the stables and w'en them 'osses sid the stoppages they fell jed."

◇   ◇   ◇

At a smoking concert a young man went onto the platform to give a song. He got through the performance with a few cat calls but no applause. When he returned to his seat the old man who sat beside him patted his shoulder and said: "Nivver thee mind, lad. I'm sewer tha's dun thee best . . . But them fowk as ivver tode thee that tha cud sing owt to be shot."

3

Couple being married. The preacher said to the girl: "will you take this man to be your lawfully wedded husband?" She said "I will."

"Repeat after me," he went on . . . "to love, honour, cherish and obey."

She said: "to luv, 'onour, cherish, bay . . ."

The preacher said: "You'll have to say obey."

The bridegroom cut in impatiently: "Goo on, let 'er say bay. I'll mek her say O when I get 'er wum."

◇　◇　◇

A busy doctor told a woman to take the temperature of her sick husband that evening and he would look in again next day. When he arrived the woman was going about her work, singing gaily.

"Well, my good woman. Did you take your husband's temperature?"

"Oh, yes sir. I put the barometer on 'is stummick an' it swung round ter very dry, so I gid 'im a pint a fourpenny an' 'e's gone ter werk this mornin'."

◇　◇　◇

Election time. A candidate called on a doubtful voter, who to his surprise said that he would give him his vote. "Glad to hear it, I'm sure," he said. "I thought you were against me."

"Arr, I wuz at fust," said the voter. "W'en th' other day yo' called 'ere an' stood by the pigstye, gabbin' fer 'arf an 'our, yo' dey budge me an inch. But after you'd gone I got ter thinkin' 'ow yo'd reached yo're 'ond over an' scratched the pig's back till 'e laid down wi' the pleasure of it, an' oi med up me mind the'er an' then that w'en a mon's as sociable as that wi' a poor creatur, oi wasna the mon ter vote agin 'im."

◇　◇　◇

"You can't keep a pig in the house. What about all the smell and filth?"

"Do yo' worry about that. The pig 'ull jest 'ave ter git used to it."

4

OUR GRANDAD'S WUM MED BREW

There wuz nothen' nowheer better
Than our grandad's wum med beer . . .
Brewed to 'iz special recipe
In our ode brewuss theer . . .

Juss the smell er that stuff a-bilen,
I used to eer et said,
Wuz enough ter knock yer 'at off —
Or spin yer eyes round in yer yed!

An' when et come ter tappen out,
Ooh! Yoe cor explain the tairst!
E'ed power et out while ee sot in the bath,
Soo az none ud goo ter wairst . . .

All the folks from miles around
Ud get ter know, an' come . . .
Even the vicar ud call ter bless et,
An' tek a drap back wum!

But the come a time az grandad's airl
Day somehow tairst the sairm . . .
Burree swore e'ed med et like before,
Soo we day know what ter blairm!

'Ee never brewed good beer again,
Nairw! Never after that . . .
'Ee lost the trick the very sairm wik
We lost our ode tum-cat!

Doug. Southall

" Frankly, I was completely bowled over "

❖   ❖   ❖

A crowd of men, singing and shouting were coming home from the pub. They stopped outside a house and were silent for a moment. Then the least drunk member of the gang shouted, " Hey, misis, come an' pick yoern outa we!"

❖   ❖   ❖

The local preacher was taking his evening stroll during a long drought. As he passed the nearest allotment a gardener said " Eh gaffer, yo'm a praycher bay yer?"

" I do indeed try to preach the word of the Lord."

" Well, why doe yer do somethin' useful and pray for rain?"

The preacher wetted his forefingers and raised his hand and then said, " Bert, es no good prayin' for rain with the wind in that direction."

❖   ❖   ❖

" Dear God, Yo' read in the paeper this mornin' about the pit accident?"

Two factory hands sitting on a low wall inside the works, eating their midday snap. Suddenly one of them fell to the ground and rolled about in agony. The other man observed him with anxiety, but without positive action.

A passerby stopped and said: " This man is ill, he ought to see a doctor," whereupon the sufferer stopped groaning for long enough to say with an air of resentment—" W'ot? In me own time?"

◇ ◇ ◇

Man retreating from a fight: " Better ter be a cowerd for a day than a jed bloke all yer life."

◇ ◇ ◇

" Why have you placed two hot water bottles in my bed, Alice?"

" Ar well, yer see, mum, one of 'em is leakin' and I don't know which, so I put both on 'um in ter mek sure."

◇ ◇ ◇

A couple of black country farmers on their way home in a dog cart after celebrating a good sale at the market:

" Ay . . . look we'er yo'm agooin', Sam. Yo' neerly 'it that 'ooman crossin' the rode."

" It's yo' as wants ter look. Yo'm drivin', bay yer."

" No I bay. I thought yo' wun!"

◇ ◇ ◇

A story from Sodom.

Billy Major Mobberley of Woodsetton always went to work on horseback to his Sodom brickworks, passing Dr. Millington's surgery on the way. A Sodom woman suffering from constipation had been attending the surgery and receiving treatment. One morning she went to see her doctor.

" Have you passed anything?" he asked.

" Ar . . . I's jest passed ode Mobley on is 'oss."

A workman was riding his bike in the middle of the tram lines when a tram comes up behind, the driver clanging his bell. Still the cyclist stuck to his course. As the tram threatened his rear mudguard the driver leaned over and shouted:

"Cosn't thee get out o' them the'er tram lines?"

"Ar," shouted the workman over his shoulder, "I con . . . but ah bet thee a quid thee cosn't."

◇   ◇   ◇

A couple of unemployed labourers were walking along to the pub one Friday night when one of them stopped suddenly and picked up a pay packet.

"Yo' bay arf lucky, ower kid," said the other enviously as he watched him open it.

"I bloody bay," said the finder in disgust. "Jest look at them stoppages."

◇   ◇   ◇

Two Wolves fans on their way to Molineux waiting at a bus stop outside a church.

"Well ahr kid. Dun yer think it's gooin' ter keep fine for we?"

"I doe 'no abaht that. Tell the trooth, I doe like the look o' that cock up the'er on the steeple."

"Arr, yo' doe want ter tek tew much notice o' that thing. The wind blows it anyweer."

◇   ◇   ◇

A simple minded youth who had secured a maintenance job with the council was seen mending a fence. Pulling a handful of nails out of his pocket, he threw a good half of them away.

"What did you do that for?" enquired a bystander.

"Cos thy'm no good, thet's why. The yeds am on the wrong end."

Bystander (having him on). "Doe waeste 'em. Goo round t'other side an' knock 'em in from the'er."

8

HOW TER GET FREE BEER AN' PAY FOR IT

YOUNG Sammy 'Sly' was thirsty, an' sweatin' like a bull,
'E dreamed o' fizzy beer an' a good long pull;
But 'e 'ad'na got no munny soo 'e 'ad a crafty think,
Then 'e went intew The Flooded Mine an' asked fer a drink,
They put the beer afore him—then Sammy gid a shout,
"Theer's tew big rats jus' scrawled in 'ere—please gerrum out!"

The women started squailin'; the landlord gorra stick
They all gor' in a turmoil soo Sammy drunk up quick,
Then outside 'e skidadled afore they knowed 'e'd gone,
It took o'de Tum the landlord some time ter cotton on,
But when 'e did 'e maird a vow ter keep a sharp look out
"Ar'll ketch 'im, doe yo' werrit, an' ar'll bost 'is snout!"

Young Sammy loffed 'is socks off at 'ow 'e'd gor' 'is beer,
An' 'e toed some mates about it, bur' 'e dae say wheer,
An' one called Screwlewse Flairvell, a listening at the back,
Though as 'ow when 'e got thairsty as 'e'd 'ave a crack
Soo a cuppla nights lairter 'bout 'arf-past nine,
'E finished 'is pub-crawlin' at ' The Flooded Mine.'

'E'd on'y gorra tanner soo 'e thought 'e'd 'ave a try,
Ter gerra drink o' beer free like Sammy ' Sly;'
'E called fer bottled Guiness an' they set 'im up a jar,
Then 'Screwlewse' gid a crafty look around the bar,
Jumps up jus' like a gawbee an' giz a great big shout—
" Theer's tew big rats jus' cum in 'ere—now gerrum out!"

Now 'e shud'na a'said that the moment when 'e did,
'Cos a couple o' tough moulders nairme o' Bill an' Sid,
'Ad jus' stepped in the doore when the wairds cum out,
An' they thought as 'Screwlewse' meant them soo they
    thumped his snout;
The landlord's bally wobbled an' 'is fairce went bright wi'
    glee,
'E cried " Now let me gi'e 'im one wi' love from me!"

J. William Jones

9

Distraught man at a graveside: " Why am yer jed? Why am yer jed?"

Passerby, sympathetically: " Is that your wife?"

"No it bloody ay. It's 'er fust 'usband."

◇   ◇   ◇

A man walked into a local pub with a very attractive large dog. They both sat down quietly and presently another man came in with a yet larger and more vicious dog. He immediately began to boast about the fighting qualities of his animal. Seeing the first man's dog, he challenged him to fight the two animals outside.

The challenge was successful and both men and dogs retired into the yard. After a few minutes the first dog returned, having killed his opponent. The amazed locals in the pub asked the owner what sort of a dog he had.

"Ah doe rightly know," he replied. "Ow'er kid went off on a trip from the werks last 'ear an' brought 'im back from Africa. Mind yo', 'e wor 'arf queer lookin'. We 'ad to shave off 'is beard to mek 'im look summat loike!"

◇   ◇   ◇

Description of a presentation watch: " All the iron in it is gold except the glass."

◇   ◇   ◇

Them ay 'arf big bay winders, bin 'em? Bay 'um?

◇   ◇   ◇

A teenage girl was swimming nude in the cut when a man came along and sat on the bank watching her. In spite of her entreaties he refused to go away and after a long time, when she was cold and tired and simply had to come out, she felt around in the water and finally came out with a frying pan held in front of her.

"Now . . ." she said furiously. "Want to know what I think . . .?"

"Yo' doe 'ave ter tell me," he said. "Yo' think the'ers a bottom in that the'er fryin' pon."

10

A carpenter working in Oldbury sent the new apprentice to the corner shop to fetch him some Park Drive cigarettes. He returned with the money, but without the cigarettes and said: "They ain't got no Park Drive."

"Bring anything, then," said the carpenter.

The apprentice came back with a pork pie.

◇　◇　◇

Cum round one o' these afternoons an' stop all day!

◇　◇　◇

Said of a woman who married a rich man and lived unhappily afterwards: " er married the miskin fer the muck an' got pizened wi' the stink!"

◇　◇　◇

At the butcher's: " Yo' mind . . . yo'm geein' me a lot a boon the'er."

"Ar bay, missus. Yo'm payin' for it."

◇　◇　◇

Two local girls arranged to meet someone at a certain place. Describing what happened afterwards, the one girl said to her boyfriend: " That's what I sed to 'er: either 'e ay cum or 'e ay 'ere."

◇　◇　◇

" I'm worried about our Emma . . . that eldest wench of owern. 'Er's so thin."

" I shouldna myther meself too much about that, Mr. Perkins. I got a cousin . . . me cousin Phoebe. 'Ere's twice as thin as yower Emma . . . an' 'er ates like an 'oss."

◇　◇　◇

The next toime as ah cum ter meet yo', ah'll stop at whum!"

11

An artless lout shouted scornfully to a down-an-out beggar: "Yo'm in a miserable condition if there bay another world."

"Arr," said the beggar. "And yo'm in a wuss condition if there bin."

◇ ◇ ◇

Discharging a man with a caution the magistrate said: "Remember, if you come here again you'll get twice as much."

◇ ◇ ◇

A man was charged with using bad language. The officer wrote down the words complained of and handed them to the defendant: "Did you use these words?" asked the clerk of the justices.

"No, I dey."

"Can you read?"

"No, I cor."

◇ ◇ ◇

Stupid farmhands watching a flight of birds. As one of the birds dived down to about a thousand feet, one of the farmhands muttered:

"Yo' look at that all this way inland. They'm gulls."

"Goo on," said his companion. "Yo' cor tell what sex they am from all this way orf."

◇ ◇ ◇

The missus ay 'arf a good un wi' the 'ousekeeping money. Yo' know, 'er went to the butcher's last wik an' bought a pound o' boones an' got tew pound o' mate off of 'em!"

◇ ◇ ◇

A child's description to her teacher of a Black Country funeral: "It was loike a weddin' Miss . . . ony wi' a box!"

AYLI'S MUNTHLY WAIRJIZ

Ayli guz fer 'iz yewshewul drink
Un wor 'arf lukkin' glum
'Iz trubbles tew 'iz pals powered aht
Abahrr 'iz life at wum.

" It's me missis wot's bin onter me
A rite bost up we'n 'ad
Ah wish 'er'd goo un drahned 'erself
'Er meks me sick un bad.

'Er's socked me wi' the rowlin' pin
Me yed—it ay 'arf sooer
Abaht munee we'n bin rowin'
'Er sez 'er waants sum mooer."

" Yow gi' 'er yer wairjiz wen yow'm payed "
Sed Aynuk sympathizin'
" 'Er orter know it ay yower fault
Uz priyciz kayp on rizin'."

" Wen ah'm payed wunce a munth," sed Ayli
" The fairm giz me a cheque
Ah tek it wum un gi' it 'er
'Er knows jus' worr ah mek.

'Er giz me a bit ter kayp fer meself
It dow buy me a lot."
" But yow'n alliz got plenty," sed Aynuk
Bags mooer thun worr ah'n got."

" But nairw yow'n gorra 'ear the wust,"
Sed Ayli all dismayed.
" 'Er's fun aht the trewth frum sumwe'er
It's evvry fortnit ah get payed."

Kate Fletcher

A schoolteacher was telling a class of infants the story of the Prodigal Son. She came to the part where the son has spent all his money and found himself starving. "And so," she said, "the poor boy had to go into the sty and eat the pig's food."

From one little angel at the back of the class came the spontaneous outburst: "The filthy sod!"

◊　◊　◊

A couple of well-to-do Black Countrymen met at the door of a psychiatrist's office in Brummagen.

"Hello" said one. "Are you coming or going?"

"If I knew that," said the other, "I wouldn't be here."

◊　◊　◊

One Sunday morning in the days of horse-drawn vehicles, a brake with ten men aboard pulled up outside a public house. A customer looking out of the window said: "I wonder where that lot come from."

The landlord took a quick look and said: "They come from Bilston."

"How do you know that?"

"Because the 'oss is the only one wearing a collar."

◊　◊　◊

Bus passenger to conductor: "We'er yo' gooin'?"

"Missus, ah doe rightly know."

"But you've got Ode 'ill on the front."

"Ah . . . an' we got India on the tyres, but we ay gooin' the'er."

◊　◊　◊

Two drunks going home along the railway line.

"This ay 'arf a bloomin' long staircase."

"I do' mind the length. It's the buggerin' low 'andrail I cor do with."

14

" Chap, ah sumtimes wish yoh'd stuck ter stamp collectin' "

❖   ❖   ❖

A local collier married a girl who had only one eye. After
a few years the collier fell to drinking and the wife to nagging, so that the relationship deteriorated. Coming home one
night from the pub, the collier was met and abused by his
wife at the door of the house. Grabbing the frying-pan which
was lying handy, he struck his wife on the head with it,
shouting: " Th'er! That'll larn yer; Now yo've got tew one
eyes!"

❖   ❖   ❖

Two workmen on a day out were looking round Dudley
Zoo. In front of the bird collection they stopped to stare at a
large bird standing on one leg.
" What's that 'un, Charlie?"
" Do yo' know? That's a stork."
" I know it's a stalk, yer fule. But what's that on top on it?"

Two men were discussing the ability of the goalkeeper of their local football team.

" 'E ay ser bad," said one, " 'e stops all the fast uns, but the slow uns goo past him loike lightnin'."

❖   ❖   ❖

"Last time I set eyes on yo', yo' were out o' sight already."

❖   ❖   ❖

After the school holiday a teacher asked one of her pupils if he had enjoyed going away to the seaside:

"It was orlright but we come back Tuesday. Me dad dey loike the breakfuses. The second mornin' when they brought the grapefruit, he said we bay staying 'ere, it's alus code."

❖   ❖   ❖

Conversation at a Wednesbury dart match:

" 'E cor 'arf throw good."

"What dun yo' expect? 'E comes from the Chuckery."

❖   ❖   ❖

"My ode 'ooman alus meks love wi' 'er eyes shut. 'Er just cor abide seein' me enjoy meself."

❖   ❖   ❖

Two women enjoying a night out at the local pub.

"Having another one?"

"No yer fule. It's the way me coote's buttoned up."

❖   ❖   ❖

Two Black Country lads out on a shoot one Saturday morning.

"Drat it, Bill. We'n bin at it all mornin' an' we ay 'it a thing."

"No more we ay. We'll just miss two more, then we'll goo whum."

Workman reporting to the foreman at 8 a.m.
" Ah'm just cum in ter tell yer that ah'm tew bad ter cum ter werk this mornin'."

◇   ◇   ◇

A well-known Wednesbury character was once asked to glaze a group of newly-built houses. When the work was not done after a month, the builder approached him and was given the reason for the delay.
" The firm as supplies the glass writ to tell me as they'd lost me address!"

◇   ◇   ◇

A Tipton man with a 'cushy' job once fell asleep whilst at work and found when he woke up that he had worked five hours overtime.

◇   ◇   ◇

" Eh, Bill, that pig as yo'm a rearin' is gooner be tew big for yo'er fambly."
" Doe yo' worry, I'n thought what ter dew. We'll kill one half this month and the t'other half next!"

◇   ◇   ◇

A man who had papered the front room of his house told a neighbour that he had bought eight rolls of paper. The neighbour decided he would do the same. Next time they met:
" Er, 'ows this, Tum? Buth our 'ouses 'um the saeme. I bought eight rolls o' paper loike yo', an' 'ad fower left over."
" Ar . . . soo did I."

◇   ◇   ◇

The comely butcher"'s wife was standing at the entrance to the shop when a local preacher, Mr. Davies, was passing on the opposite side of the road. In a loud voice she cried: " I'll have a nice clean belly for you tonight, Mr. Davies."

❖ ❖ ❖

A couple retired to bed, but instead of going to sleep the man tossed and turned, obviously very worried.

"What's the marrer, me luv? Why cor yer goo ter slape?'

"' I moight as well tell yer, Sally. I borrered £5 from the neighbour opposite and I cor pay it back. I've sode me whippet. I ay got nothun' else.''

The wife promptly gets out of bed, opens the window and shouts across the street. "Yo 'ear over the'er! Know that £5 we'n borrered? Well, we cor pay it back."

She slammed down the window and returned to bed. " Now let's get ter slape an' let them do the worryin'.''

❖ ❖ ❖

In one of the old houses on Monmore Green, a man was helping the doctor at the delivery of his latest offspring by holding the oil lamp. When the doctor had produced first one, then two babies and was still busily occupied, the man suddenly bolted out of the room.

"Come back with that lamp," shouted the doctor.

"I shore. It's that bloody light that's attractin' 'em.''

ODE GEORGE

Ode George—'e wor a skoller
'E cudn't rayd nor rite
Soo thort 'e'd ejercairt izself
Un gurra skewl ut nite.

Soo wen 'iz mind wuz all med up
'E payed 'iz entrunss fee
Un serr abaht this jiyunt task
Ter lairn 'iz A.B.C.

Not menny wiks ud passed by
Wen George cud rayd quite well
Burr az 'e tried ter rite wairds dahn
It puzzled 'im ter spell.

'E cudn't gerr it in 'iz yed
Abahrr a waird quite small
Soo thort 'e'd ask a bloke ut wairk
If 'e'd explairn it all.

Then wen 'e cum across 'iz mairt
George asked 'im if 'e knew
Why the'er wuz ser menny ways
O' spellin' this waird tew.

Olf explained uz best 'e cud
Un spelt the waird T.O.
" That's mayns wen yow gu sumwe'er
Like gooin' tew a show."

Then next 'e spelt aht T.O.O.
Which Olf sed ment also
" Un then o' course theer'z number 2
Yow spell T.W.O."

George thanked Olf fer explairnin'
But still appayered in daht
'E porzed awile then sed t' Olf
" Theer's one that thee'st left aht

Yow ay much gud ut taychin'
This less'n ay cumplete
Thee 'as'nt tode me 'ow yow spell
The tooz wot's on yer feet."

Kate Fletcher

◆　◇　◆

" If yoh ay the one 'oo's bin pinchin' the deck-cheers, yoh
woh mind bein' sairched, wull yoh?"

A schoolboy was asked to write about something that had happened at home. He wrote: Last night mum and dad went to the pictures. A girl came to babysit and her boyfriend came as well and they got married on the rug.

❖   ❖   ◆

Businessman to secretary as traveller leaves: " I cor stand a liar. Next time he comes tell 'im I'm out."

◇   ◇   ◇

" I'm lookin' forward to Christmas remarked a Jewish friend of a Blackcountry man. "Ah dey think yo' Jews celebrated that," said the local man.
" O, yes. After all, Jesus was a Jew."
" Ah, but ony on 'is mother's side!"

◇   ◇   ◇

A woman had promised to go out with a friend one evening. When the time came to start she didn't want to go.
Her husband said: " Well, whoy doh yoh go rahnd arid tell 'er as yo' cor cum?"

◇   ◇   ◇

I dreamt I was dead and to heaven did go,
" Where did you come from?" they wanted to know;
I said: "I'm from Bilston,"
St. Peter did stare;
Says he: " Walk right in you're the first one from there."

◇   ◇   ◇

Notice outside a black country factory: **Special Short Shifts For Married Men.**

◇   ◇   ◇

Tenant complaining about a council house: " I had to paint the ceiling blue because when it was white it looked black all the time."

I dey think it was easy ter tek pictures in colour 'till I sid 'em in black an' white.

◇ ◇ ◇

A Gornal man returned to his native village after an absence of many years, and dropped into a neighbouring pub for a pint. After introducing himself to the landlord he was asked if the old place had changed much.

"Yes . . . that 'ill over the'er used to 'ave tew windmills, now there's ony one!"

"Yo'm right! We fun there wore enuff wind fer tew on 'em, so we pulled one down!"

◇ ◇ ◇

Official to widow: "Now you fill in this form here, here and here. Did your husband die intestate?"

Widow: "No, 'e day. 'E died in Smethwick."

◇ ◇ ◇

"An' yo' heerd the latest about the mines?"

"Now, wa' is it?"

"Mine's a bitter!"

◇ ◇ ◇

Foreman: "Now then, Bill, wot about carryin' sum moer bricks?"

Workman: "I cor, gaffer. I bay well. I'm a tremblin' all over."

Foreman: "Well then. Get busy wi' that the'er sieve."

◇ ◇ ◇

Workman: "I do' waent ter carry a 'od all me life, I waent ter wheel a barrer."

Foreman: "Yo'! Wheel a barrer? Wor done yo' know about machinery?"

◇ ◇ ◇

It's as code outside as it is in the street.

A man was building a fowl run in his garden when his mate called to see him. "Affore yo' tell me what yo'n cum abaht, what dun yer think o' me fowl run wi' the new wire nettin' I got on it?"

"It's orlright ower kid. But wo' the fowl git wet? It'll raen in, wo' it?"

"It wo'. Not w'en I've dun. I'm agooin' ter slope the run a bit moer."

Caller: " How's business these days?"
Businessman: " S'awful! Things bin so bad that even them wot do' pay an' stopped sendin' we orders."

◇   ◇   ◇

Jack was taking a last look at his pal who had died suddenly.

" He's got a happy smile," he commented to his friend's wife.

" Ah, yes," she said, sadly. " That's because he died in his sleep. He doesn't know he's gone yet."

◇   ◇   ◇

" Yoer new babby ay a very big un' is 'e?"

" Well, wot dun yer expect. Me an 'is faether 'ave ony been married three months!"

◇   ◇   ◇

" I like yer new coat."

" Ar, genuine simulated mink."

" Cost yer a bit day et?"

" Day cost me anythin'—Gaffer took me to 'is 'ouse after the Christmas Party and gied et me—for nuthin'."

" O ar, what did yer 'ave ter do?"

" On'y shorten the sleeves a bit!"

◇   ◇   ◇

" A comb please."

" Do you want a steel one?"

" No, I'll pay for it."

◇   ◇   ◇

" Wot's the boss like at thet new place where you'n just started?"

" 'E's bloody saft! 'E aksed me three times w'ere me 'at was, an' it was on me yed all the time."

24

IN STYLE

They says yome fat, yer chest's too flat—
They tells yer that—but ar doe!

Or yome too thin—all boon and skin—
Yoe just cor win!—but ar doe!

These fashion models posen
Fer photographs in books,
Convinced as they'm the ideal shairp
In figure an' in looks!

Yoe siz um on the telly—
A-prancen' up an' down . . .
" And here Diane is wearing
An organdie evening-gown!"

The very chic, and latest trend,
Created by Deveele
Accessories, handbag to match
" With coiffeure by Cecille."

Oon they think they'm kidden, kid,
All dressed up to a tee . . . ?
Looken just like jeth warmed up
Doe do a thing fer me!

Nairw! gime women as is nature's shairp!
Wi' real smiles on their fairces!
Ooo bulges, an' lets it all 'ang out
In thode familiar plairces!

Oh yes mar wench! Real style—real class,
When yoe faircen up to facts
Ay the way yoe look—or dress,
It's simply how yoe acts!

Doug. Southall

The ranter in the old Primitive Methodist Chapel was in fine form.

"Come the day of judgement" he yelled "an' there will be weepin' an' wailin' an' gnashin' o' teeth."

"Gaffer, 'ow about them 'as 'ay got no teeth?"

"Teeth will be provided!"

◇　◇　◇

"I 'ave ter drink me beer quick cos I once 'ad a' accident."

"Yo've never 'ad a' accident in yer life!"

"I ave. I once 'ad a pint knocked over."

◇　◇　◇

"'Ow dun yer like me new frock?"

"It looked better wen the taerters wun in it!"

◇　◇　◇

The smart Birmingham man had just married a Gornal girl and they were about to spend their first night together at the honeymoon hotel. Thinking his new bride might be a little shy he said "Now my dear, if you would like to go up to our bedroom and—er—get ready, I'll be upstairs in about 20 minutes."

After 20 minutes he enters the bedroom to find his bride fully dressed—hat, fur coat, walking shoes—the lot.

"But—but—I thought you would be in bed," he stammered, but the girl said: "My mother told me as yo' Brummies always went to town on the fust night an' I thought I'd come with yer!"

◇　◇　◇

"Dun yo' know 'im Ayli?"

"No, never sid 'im afore."

"Dun yo' know 'im Tummy?"

"No, I do know 'im either."

"Chuck arf a brick at 'im then."

◇　◇　◇

It ay stopped rainin' since it started.

A well known Black Country character had earned quite a reputation by being able to recognise any beer or wine or spirit even when they were mixed. Five or six wines would be mixed with three or four different beers and he would win bets by naming each individual drink. One Christmas his friends decided to play a trick on him. They persuaded the pub landlord to give him a glass of water and his friends bet him he would not recognise it.

The boozer took several sips each time looking more and more puzzled and at length said:

"Well mates, yo've got me beat at last. I've never taested anythin' like that in my life. I doe know what it is but I'll tell yer one thing. It'll never sell!"

◇   ◇   ◇

"'ow's yer dog?"

"Jed."

"What was the matter wi' 'im?"

"Flu."

"Dogs doe 'ave flu."

"Mine did. 'E flew under a 'bus."

◇   ◇   ◇

The Dudley policeman was amazed to see the old car going around and around the traffic island. After the 86th circuit he thought perhaps the driver was drunk so he strode into the road and held up his hand. The car stopped and this conversation too place.

"Now my man what's the idea? I've been watching you drive around this island nearly ninety times. What are you playing at?"

"Well I cor 'elp it mate if me indicator's stuck con I?"

◇   ◇   ◇

"What 'ave yer got yer foot bandaged up for?"

"'Cos I cut it bad."

"'Ow?"

"I was watchin' some steeplejacks mend a chimney and one of 'em dropped a brick right on my yed. I think I was standin' on some glass at the time."

STOP IT ADA

"STOP it Ada—stop it wut?
Yo'm gie'in' me a pain in the gut!
Ar'm a'gerrin' all wairked up ar bin
Like liver-salts wi' a wet-spewn in,
Stop dewin' it—I asks yer now—
Cor yer see the swat beadin' on me brow?"

"Stop it Ada! No—carry on!
Ar'm a helpless, hopeless, yewseless mon;
Yo'n jus' got me wheer yo' want me see?
A tewl in the 'onds o' such as thee;
Stop dewin' it—O'doe be crewil!
Ar feel like ar'm sinkin' in coed wet grewil."

"Stop it Ada! Well . . . . alright!
Jus' once moore then as it's Friday night;
Ar doe know wor' ar'sll dew ar'm shewer,
The years o' life get fewer an' fewer,
An' yo' gorra lood 'em up wi' pleasure,
Else they gerrin tew long fer yo' ter measure."

"Now that's it Ada! No moore!
Ar shor be airble ter cross this floore;
Ar've toed yer—ar'm a weak 'elpless mon,
Jus'—'TEW MOORE TAIRTERS OUT'A THE PON
AN P'RAPS ANOTHER CHOP WHILE YO'M THEER
AN' JUS' ONE MOORE PINT O' YO'RE UM-BREWED
BEER.'"

Jim William Jones

The fire brigade watched by the inevitable crowd, were fighting a fire in an old three storey house. Suddenly a woman holding a tiny baby appeared at the topmost window. The firemen produced a large blanket held by ten brawny men.

" Jump missis," they shouted.

" What about me babby?"

" Throw 'im down fust."

" I'm frightened I shall miss the blanket an' 'e'll be killed."

" Yo'll both be killed if yo' doe do summat quick."

In spite of the firemen's efforts the flames got worse when a man stepped out from the crowd.

" Missis, yo' throw yer babby down an' I'll ketch 'im. I'm the Albion goalkeeper an' I've never missed a ball yet. Goo on throw 'im down."

The woman threw the baby and with a great effort the goalie skilfully caught him. There was a great cheer from the crowd. The goalkeeper then kicked the baby 100 yards up the street!

◇　　◇　　◇

" That bloke ay 'arf unlucky."

" Why?"

" 'E bought 500 aspirins to commit suicide, took a couple an' felt better."

◇　　◇　　◇

'Lijah the poacher had taken a duck from the local pond for his family's Sunday dinner. Plucking it in a hedge near the pond he was surprised by a policeman.

" Poachin' agen 'Lijah?" he said.

" No gaffer, I'm on'y 'odin 'is clothes while he goes for a swim!"

◇　　◇　　◇

" That bloke's drunk!"

" Ow con yer tell?"

" I can see two of 'im!"

◇　　◇　　◇

" Gaffer am yo' sure this fish is cooked? 'E's et nearly all my chips!"

Ayli is in the butchers one morning when suddenly in dashes a large dog, picks up a joint of beef and dashes out.

"Ayli wor that yo'er dog?" said the butcher.

"Well gaffer, 'e used ter be but 'e looks after himself now " said Ayli.

◇　◇　◇

"I see yo've been fightin' agen. Who was it this time?"

"I 'ad a few words wi' Big Mike next door. I said some nasty things about the Pope."

"Well yo' must be daft. Big Mike's twice yoer size an' yo' knowen 'e's a Catholic."

"I know Big Mike is but I day know the Pope was!"

◇　◇　◇

"We 'ad a fairy-taerle Christmas we did."

"'ow dun yer mean?"

"Grimm!"

◇　◇　◇

"Faether. I've plucked the chicken and stuffed it but I doe think it's jed yet."

◇　◇　◇

Many visitors used to come to Cradley Heath when it was famous for the manufacture of chain. On one occasion a young woman found it necessary to visit a doctor well known for his bluntness. He examined the lady and then said " Well Mrs. Jones there is nothing seriously wrong with you, but you are pregnant."

"I am not Mrs. Jones, I am Miss Jones so you must be wrong " she said.

"I cor 'elp that " said the doctor, " whether yo' are a Miss or not is your business but yo're still pregnant."

"But it's still impossible doctor. I am engaged but my fiancé and I only make love with our eyes."

"Well, your fiancé must be cock-eyed!"

FIRECAN DAYS

Did yoe ever swing a firecan round
When yoe wuz a little mite?
Full er gleads fresh off the bonk,
Mekken sparks fly in the night?

Did yer play wi' tops an' whips,
Newspairper kites a-flyen,
Jack upon a mopstick by thode lamp,
Ad a fight an' gone wum cryen?

Aar bout a gairm er kick can nurkey,
Or marbles in the gutter,
Aten bread yer mother spread
Wi' lard cos the wor no butter . . .?

Pocket-money a penny a wik,
In 'arf 'our et ad gone . . .
Shared yer suck with all yer mates,
Cos 'arf on um never 'ad none . . .

Did yer swim in the cut with all thode gang,
Mek slides when the roads wun froze?
Gerra snowball down yer neckole
As knocked the dewdrap off yer nose?

Ef yoe knowen wha' arm on about,
An in yer mem'ry still cun see
Them things yoe did when yoe wuz a kid,
Then yoe day live ser fur from me!

Doug. Southall

At the local Derby—Wolves v Albion, a Wolves supporter was standing next to an Albion supporter who had with him a large dog. Albion scored a goal and the dog stood on his hind legs and clapped his front paws.

"Does he always do that?" asked the Wolves man.

"'Ar I allus teks 'im into a match an' 'e allus claps 'is paws wen th' Albion scores."

"Wot's 'e do if the Wolves score?"

"O 'e rolls over an' over."

"'Ow many times?"

"Depends on 'ow 'ard I kick 'is arse!"

◆ ◆ ◆

Coming from a pub in Dudley, Joey the puddler was amazed to see an elephant come out of the zoo, smash a jeweller's window, suck up jewels and watches in his trunk and then trot back to the zoo. Still amazed, Joey went to the police station to report the occurrence. The policeman took down his statement and then said, "Now my man was it an Indian elephant or an African elephant?"

"'Ow the 'ell should I know?"

"Well the African has big ears and the Indian small ones."

"Ar but this one had a stockin' over 'is yed."

◆ ◆ ◆

"Ay gaffer 'ould yo' like a good time?"

"Clear off yer cheeky madam. In any case I've on'y got a 50p piece."

"That's all right. I've got plenty o' change."

◆ ◆ ◆

Joshua was a first class toolmaker and he had worked for a rather mean gaffer for many years. On one occasion he was called to the office and showed a very complicated drawing.

"Now, I want you to make a tool to them specifications Josh."

"I cor mek a tool for that gaffer—et's impossible. An' if I cor mek et there ay a bloke in the world es can mek it. Yo'll 'ave ter buy one!"

32

The final and decisive domino game was being played in a Wednesbury match. An onlooker was asked how the game was going.

"Oh, it's a front room" was the reply.

The speaker wanted to say that so far it was a drawn game, with both sides equal. It was, then, like 'our front room'— there was nothing in it!

❖   ❖   ❖

A Black Countryman had at last been sent to Heaven. He rang the bell at the Pearly Gates and out came St. Peter. "I'm afraid you'll have to go to the other place, my man" he said "we can't make grorty pudding for one up here."

❖   ❖   ❖

"Lewk, Olf! Yoh con see the say"

❖   ❖   ❖

"Yo' can allus tell ets summer cor yer?"
"Wot! in weather like this?"
"Ar, the rain's warmer!"

33

Tommy the collier and his wife kept a small general dealer's shop in Cradley Heath. Mrs. Tommy became very ill and the family gathered around the bedside expecting her to die.

"Doe yo' forget, our Tummy, when I'm jed that owd Widder Brown as now lives up Barrs Bonk owes me five shillings since last Christmas" she whispered.

"'Ark at 'er" said Tommy, "marvellous ay 'er? Sensible to the last."

"An' doe yo' forget our Tummy 'as we owes Mr. Hingley £2 for coal."

"Now 'ers a-mitherin', Tek no notice on 'er" Tommy advised his family.

◊　◊　◊

The 'bus stopped outside the 'Green Dragon' where a Gornal woman with about 14 children were waiting for it to take them to Wolverhampton.

"Now them two theer am on'y 14 and they'm twins. Half fare for them ay et?

"An' them two theer am 13 and they'm twins" and so she obtained half fare for all of them claiming each pair were twins.

"Bin all them yoern?" asked the puzzled driver.

"Course they bin."

"Well dun yo 'ave twins every time?"

"No, sometimes we dow 'ave no kids at all."

◊　◊　◊

"Well, ef et ay Emily Turner. I ay sid yo' for 10 years at least. 'Ow am yer gerrin' on?"

"Not tew bad. I've gorrer council flat now an ets very comfortable. Yo' know me 'usband died though doe yer?"

"No, I day. 'Ow did 'e die?"

"O, ever so sudden. 'E'd got an allotment an' every Sunday 'e'd goo up theer and fetch summat for we Sunday dinner. One Sunday 'e day cum back an' at 3 o'clock I went up the allotment to see wot was up. When I got theer I 'ad a terrible shock. Theer 'e was—jed—in the salary trench.

"That must a bin 'orrible fer yer. What did yer do?"

"I opened a can o' pays!"

FAIRTHER-LAW

Arn gorra smoshen' fairther-law!
Iss right! Ar thinks eez great!
Closer than a brother is—
In fact, eez mar best mate!

Eez a mon yoe c'n depend on,
Whenever yome in doubt . . .
Thuz oney one thing puzzles me—
Ar just cort figure out.

Why did 'ee in a blairmless life,
Av the rotten, stinken luck,
When out ter choose 'imself a wife,
Goo an' pick the one 'ee puck!

Doug. Southall

❖　　❖　　❖

**" Yoh'm sairposed ter raise the little finger uv the 'ond yohm
drinkin' with . . ."**

35

Ayli's love life had deteriorated rather badly and he went to talk over the matter with his local doctor.

"Now Ayli" said the doctor, "have you tried this method —and that method—and cut your beer drinking down and—

"I've tried all them," said Ayli. "I've even changed me Banks's to Hansons but it meks no difference. Me missus ay 'arf a' carrying on!"

"Now here's a new method being tried in the United States and some doctors say it works," said the doctor. "It's quite simple. You jog 10 miles a day for a fortnight. Then you should be back to normal!"

"O.K. I'll try it" said Ayli.

"Good. Ring me up in a fortnight or so and tell me if it worked."

Just over a fortnight later the doctor's telephone rang.

"Yo' remember me doe yer? the bloke you tode ter jog 10 miles a day for a fortnight."

"Yes of course I do" said the doctor. "Now, has it worked? Is your sex life any better?"

"Ow the 'ell do I know" yelled Ayli, "I'm 140 miles away from whum!"

◇　◇　◇

"I doe think that new school my young kid goes to is enny good at all."

"What makes yer think that?"

"They mek 'im spell taerters wi' a 'p'!"

◇　◇　◇

"Mother, I doe think me 'usband loves me as much as 'e used to."

"Wot dun yer mean?"

"Well 'e doe seem near as keen as 'e used ter be."

"Well yo' can soon cure 'im yer know."

"Ow?"

"Like I did wi' yer faether wen 'e started to lose interest. Give 'im a dozen fresh oysters afore yo' go's ter bed."

The next day the mother asked her daughter if the scheme had worked successfully.

"Yo' gied 'im the 12 oysters then day yer?"

"Yes mom, but on'y nine of 'em worked!"

Ayli was passing his old friend's, Aynuk's house when torrential rain started. He dashed in for what he thought would be a few minutes, but the rain got even worse. Soon the drains just couldn't cope and flood water swirled through the house. Eventually the two friends, with a couple of umbrellas found themselves on the roof of the house. And still the rain continued. Many houses and sheds were badly flooded and looking at the scene of destruction Aynuk said—

"Bloody awful ay et? Ay that Mrs. Hackett's fowl pen floatin' away down theer?"

"Et looks like it," said Ayli.

"Eh, Ayli, yoer bungalow 'as got a yeller roof asn't et?"

"Ar et 'as."

"Well et looks ter me as though that's yoer bungalow floatin' be'ind the fowl pen."

"No, et cor be my bungalow. I got the kay in mi pocket."

❖   ❖   ❖

During a busy morning shopping, old Liza Jane had bought a large chamber pot for the bedroom. Her last call was at the butcher's and she placed the pot on the counter and said

"A pound o' fillet."

"Five pounds yo' doe!" said the butcher.

❖   ❖   ❖

"Tablet o' soap please."

"Do you want it scented?"

"No I'll tek it with me."

❖   ❖   ❖

"An yer 'eard Mary's babby was born with a glass eye?"

"I bay surprised. 'Is faether had a crystal ball."

❖   ❖   ❖

"What did yo' 'ave fer Christmas?"

"Nuthin'."

"Why?"

"I asked me faether for an encyclopaedia an' 'e said I could walk ter school like the rest o' the kids!"

An ironworker decided to have his photograph taken at a local shop.

"How many photographs do you want?" he was asked.

"Ony one," he replied. "A big 'un ter 'ang on the wall."

"In that case," said the photographer, "I suppose you'd like it mounted."

"Oh ah," was the answer, "that's orlright, the missus ay never sid me on 'ossback."

◇　◇　◇

Black Country description of modern dancing: Shairkin' backuds an' forruds an' squaylin'!

◇　◇　◇

The bridegroom was drunk when he arrived at the church. Said the disgusted vicar to the bride: "Get him to come back when he's sober."

Bride: "I bay. When 'e's sober I cor get 'im to come at all."

◇　◇　◇

"..AN' THEN SHE TRIES TER TELL
ME I SPEND TOO MUCH TIME
ON THE ALLOTMENT AN' 'AS
'OW IT AIN'T GOOD FER ME"...

38

Just after the last war a high ranking Russian spy had been ordered to find out exactly what was going on at Tipton. Details had been carefully worked out and he had been told his contact would be Ayli and the password would be " The snow is deep in Moscow." Alighting from the train at the Owen Street station he asked the ticket collector—" Vhere iss Ayli pliss?"

" Which Ayli dun yer want mate? There's lots of Ayli's round 'ere. Dun yer want Ayli the puddler, Ayli the chainmaker, Ayli-up-the-bonk—or . . . As a matter of fact my naeme's Ayli."

The spy thought perhaps he would make a start with Ayli the ticket collector.

" Ze snow is deep in Moscow " he said.

" Et must be Ayli the spy yo' want en. 'E lives next door to the Nag's Head just up the 'igh street " said the ticket collector.

◇   ◇   ◇

After a hot day in the foundry and a few pints in the dinner break, three of the men decided they could not face work that afternoon and so they lay down for a nap by the side of the canal in Tipton.

Suddenly, two of them were woken up by the other. " Eh! look " he shouted, " see that trilby moving down the cut!"

" It ay movin'," said one of his friends, " chuck a stick at it!"

The third man did so, hit the hat, and was surprised when a hand popped out of the water. " Con yo' tell me if ah'm alright for Dudley?" asked the man in the canal.

" Ah! Carry straight on, but yo'd be better off walkin' over the fields an' takin' a short cut."

" No," came the reply. " Ah cor do that, ah'm on me bike!"

FOR TWO PINS

Thuz nobody perfect in this world—
No shairp thass all divine . . .
So why dun they pick ter ridicule
These two bow-legs er mine . . .?

Ar cort 'elp it if ar looks
Like oss-shoe upside down,
Or a cowboy az is saddle-sooer
After riden inter town.

They'n supported me all the way, this pair,
An' never put one foot wrong . . .
So arm a-stonden up fer them,
Like I av done—all along!

They c'n ride a bike, an' dance, an' 'ike,
An' run an' jump woss mooer . . .
An' let yer wheel a barrer through
Wi' two feet on the flooer!

Weem the best er mates, the three on us,
An' when trouble comes in view,
We stonds our ground an' fairces et,
An' lets it goo on through!

Call me a wishboon — are doe care!
Arm 'appy with mar lot!
Knockneed or straight — yoe c'n keep yars mate!
Arl stick ter the two arn got!

Doug. Southall

After the night before:
"Yedaerke? I 'ad ter walk round the bedroom three times affore I could lift me yed off the piller."

◊ ◊ ◊

"I ay never bin any good, but ah'm a damn site better than yo'."

◊ ◊ ◊

"I alus tek a day off every birthday."
"That's nuthin'. My missus teks a year off hers."

◊ ◊ ◊

"Ah cor get abaht the way ah oost tew"

◊ ◊ ◊

Patient to doctor: "Every toime I bend forward an' stretch out me 'onds an' mek a semi-circular movement wi' me arms, I get a chronic pain in me left shoulder."
"But why make such motions?"
"Why dun I? Dun yo' know any other way ter get into an overcoat?"

◊ ◊ ◊

"Am yo' puttin' it around that ah'm saft?"
"Why? Did yer want to keep it a secret?"

" 'Ad a bloke cum't work wi' once " said the old bricklayer. "It were 'is fust time in the buildin' trade, so ah put 'im on the concrate mixer knockin' up compo. Ah showed 'im ow to goo on and watched 'im for a minit ta mek sure 'e'd got th'idea.

Well, every time 'e chucked a shuvel a sond in, 'e shuvs the blade on it right inside the drum. Three times ah tode 'im about it, but did th' noggin-yed tek any notice? Not 'im. 'Goo on then me mon,' ah thought, 'plaze thee self, yo'll lern afore 'long.'

Sure a nuff, 'e aves in sum grav'l an' the shuvel gets 'renched out a 'is 'ond doe it! A'sted a jumpin' out a th' road, the fule stonds theer a gawpin'; around gus th' drum an' th' shuvel wi' it; up cum th'ondle an' giz 'im such a clout under th'earole. •

Afore 'e 'as th' sense t' shift — around cums th'ondle agen an' giz 'im a nuther which knocks 'im flat. Funniest thing I ever sid! Loff! Ah thought me belly 'ud bost!"

❖   ❖   ❖

Eli and Enoch were calling for their mate Joe to go to the local. •.

"Weem in luck tonight—weem's got an extermination order," says Eli.

"Oh" says Joe, "and what might that be?"

"Well," says Eli, "weem open an hour after weem shut."

❖   ❖   ❖

Billy was on the cadge as usual, and had found someone with a sympathetic ear, from whom he had managed to borrow some cash.

Seeing that Billy's dog, a bull terrier, was due to have a litter, the provider of the loan said he would accept a pup instead of repayment of his money.

No pup arrived, so the man went to call on Billy, who told him "I sold them all 'cept yourn, and it died!"

"Not bad, wench, not bad . . . dun yoh dew any strippin'?"

❖ ❖ ❖

" 'Ello, ower kid. Ow yer bin doin'?"

" Since I sid yo' me an' the ode 'ooman have got a divorce."

" Goo on? Wot 'appened to the 'ouse yo' said was in yower naeme an' 'er'n?"

" We shared it fifty-fifty."

" Ow the 'ell did yer manage ter dew that?"

" T'wor no trouble. 'Er tuk the inside an' I got the outside."

❖ ❖ ❖

Visiting curate: " It's good to pray. Prayers are messages to God."

Householder: " Is that why we send 'em at night . . . to get the cheap rate?"

❖ ❖ ❖

Overheard in a local pub: " Ah, 'e's a right bad un. One day the Lord ull drop 'is clog on 'im."

The following pages contain items from "Black Country Stories and Sketches" by John Freeman, published in 1930.

They are reproduced here by permission of his son, J. Gilbert Freeman. The original headings have been retained.

DARLASTON YARNS

THE CLINKING TOAD

BETWEEN the Black Country towns there was in the early Nineteenth Century, a constant warfare of wordy banter, which often took the form of tantalising stories.

One of these was about an old man, who was known as the wise old man of Darlaston. A man who went across the fields from Bilston to Darlaston lost his watch on the way. In those days such articles were comparatively rare anywhere, and were said to be quite unknown in Darlaston.

The Darlaston man who found it was greatly puzzled, and absolutely afraid to touch it. Hurrying back home he brought others, but they were no wiser than he. One after another they looked at it as it lay on the ground, but no one dared to pick up the mysterious thing. Then it was agreed to fetch the "wise man," whom they consulted about all dark and difficult matters. Too old and infirm to walk, they brought him in the homely wheelbarrow. The ancient man looked hard at the watch, listened to its wonderful tick and then said:

"Wheel me round it lads." They wheeled him round it.

"Wheel me round again lads," he said, looking and listening intently.

"Wheel me round again lads," he commanded once more, and when they had taken him round once again, he said with an awed voice:

"Stop lads, it's a clinking, clanking tooad, come to destroy all Darlas'on, kill it lads kill it," and with sticks and stones they "killed" it.

THE BULL-CLUB

THE members of a bull-club, who regularly brought their animals to the bull stake, and there baited them, used at times to turn them out to grass. Several were stolen from their meadow—it was supposed by Willenhall men—as the grazing land was on the Willenhall side.

After the third bull had disappeared, the rank and file members of the club began to suspect their own managers of trickery, and arranged for two of their number to watch the field on a certain night. Possibly they had over-primed themselves, for both fell asleep under a hedge, and again the thieves drove away the bull.

The next time they determined not to be outwitted. On every side of the meadow they white-washed the hedge, so that they could be quite sure of the field, and discover where the beast was driven through—the gate being locked. In the night, however, it rained heavily, and they had to give up their vigil and go home. By morning the hedges were washed quite clean, and when they came, they could find neither the bull, nor the field.

A SAUVE OLD TRADESMAN

John Petty was a chemist. He was a sauve courteous old man, who added to his kindly ways a touch of wholesome humour. One day a woman entering his shop, asked:

"Mr. Petty, will you please give me a bit of string?"

Handing her the string-box he said: "There, take what you want."

She pulled at it a long time, and Mr. Petty began to smile, and asked: "Have you got enough?"

"Yes, thank you, Mr. Petty," she answered.

"Then let me look at it, will you?" he asked, and taking it, measured it along his counter, reckoning thirty six yards. Breaking into a hearty roar, he said: "There, you've got thirty-six yards, the length of a woman's conscience."

WITTICISMS

Mr. Norris Best—known as Noddy Best—found the wit of the Gornal woman quite pungent enough for him. Mr. Best was then a magistrate, and Gornal cases were then tried at the King's Arm inn, Bilston. He was blessed with a nose that was unkindly spoken of as "pugged," and after the manner of the times wore his hair over his ears. He loved his little joke, and thought to poke a bit of fun at the old body from Gornal who came as witness. Said he with a mischievous smile:

"Betty, they tell me there are a good many donkeys at Gornal, is that so?"

"Not so maney as theer was, sir," answered the woman readily.

"How is that?" he asked.

"Well you see, sir, they've covered their ears, an' pugged their noses, an' made magistrates o' some on 'em, sir, so theer aint so maney as theer was."

◆ ◆ ◆

The wealthy ironmasters who bore the name of a familiar little bird, are reputed to have suffered many inconvenient jokes in consequence. One piquant instance is said to have occurred at the works which stood on the site of the present steel works. The principal, returning after a brief absence, saw a new labourer, who annoyed him by his "linty" movements. "Come, my man, stir yourself!" he said as he passed. The man regarded him with indifference, except that he took a sly look at his master's face, of which the most remarkable feature was his prominent nose. Looking angrily at the man, he asked sharply:

"Do you know who I am? My name is Sparrow!"

"I dey know thee wust a Sparrer, but I thought thee wast a bird o' some sort by thee bake," replied the daring joker.

Another member of the same family, who was responsible for the building of some furnaces near Stow Heath, one day asked one of the men busy on work at the erection:

"Why do they leave these holes in the furnace walls?" when the fellow slyly answered:

"Them holes bin plasen for the Sparrers to build their nesses in, sir."

There was about Bilston a droll old labourer whose singular appearance and dry sayings often caused remark. One day his employer said:

"B. you are shackling again. It doesn't seem to matter what I say to you. It appears I can't make you work."

"Yo' cor, gaffer—I cor mak' myself work, let alone yo'," was the characteristic reply.

On another occasion—a day in the country, in summer time his master had to give him a similar rebuke, when he answered with an injured air:

"How con ee work, gaffer, when the birds bin a whistlin' all o'er the place?"

Another time when he had been reproached for too readily accepting proffered refreshments, he said:

"Gaffer, I lose a good many things through not being axed to have 'em, but I never lose nothin' through sayin' no, when I bin axed."

◊   ◊   ◊

Old "Cag," a well-known collier, helped to carry a comrade who had been killed in the mines to Sedgley for interment. To the annoyance of the funeral party the grave prepared was not large enough. "Cag," the man of resource, threw off his coat and persisted in digging another grave, in which they laid the coffin. The grave-digger, sullen and angry, asked:

"What bin I gooin' to do wi' this other grave, I'd like to know?"

Pointing to the first one "Cag" turned on him a look of contempt and chuckled out:

"Keep it for theeself, mon, keep it for theeself."

◊   ◊   ◊

UNCONSCIOUS HUMOUR

UNCONSCIOUS humour in both incident and speech was an everyday feature in the life of the people. A boy was carrying a big bottle of "lowance beer" to a pit at Ladymoor. An old miner who was passing said:

"My lad, let's have a taste o' that drink, wut?"

The lad true to the tradition, replied:

"All right, but dunna thee drink much."

47

The fellow lifted the great bottle to his lips, and "swigged" away until the lad grew afraid, and shouted:

"Gaffer, dunna drink it all!"

But the man drank on, and the youngster gave a violent pull at his jacket, crying:

"Gaffer dost hear? thee'st had enough."

The man stopped drinking, and looked at him.

"Has'na heerd me a shoutin' at thee?" the lad asked in astonishment.

"No my lad I'm deef when I'm drinkin'."

◇　◇　◇

Jack Jones, an old coal-jagger, was well-known for a certain habit. As the day wore on Jack took in pint after pint, until unfit for further business, when he would curl up in the bottom of his cart, and his sagacious old horse would take him safely home.

Some local wags saw an opportunity for a neat practical joke. Stopping the horse one evening, they looked in the cart, and found Jack as usual in a deep, drunken sleep. Quickly they put up the stands, and unharnessing the animal led it away. After a while Jack awoke, stood up and looked around. Close by were some of the tricksters, waiting to see how Jack would take it. His astonishment was unmistakable. As he looked at the empty shafts, and could nowhere see his horse, he said:

"Well, if I'm Jack Joones I've lost a hoss, an' if I bey Jack Joones I've fun' a cart."

◇　◇　◇

Old Mr. Gray the chemist had a great vogue in old Bilston. His shop on Swan Bank was the resort of numbers whose faith in his medical skill was remarkable. Many stories are told of his facetious ways. A big collier chap went to have a troublesome tooth removed. "Open your mouth" said the little man in his sharp way. The fellow opened an enormous mouth, the size of which evidently surprised Mr. Gray, who said:

"Stop, stop! that's wide enough, I'm not going to stand inside it."

◇　◇　◇

An old Sinker, who was well-known about Moorcroft, was more than a bit of a wag. There were in those days old cottages scattered amongst the pit banks. Some of these were

48

rendered more picturesque because of the fantastic angles to which the mines had drawn them. One of these leaned as much as the crooked house at Himley, and his master said to him one day:

"Tom if thee cost mak' theeself comfortable in the cottage yonder, thee be's welcome to do so; I'll charge thee no rent."

"All right, gaffer, it ud suit me, an' I'd be glad to save the bit o' rent," replied Tom.

Meeting him some time after he had settled in his new home, his master asked:

"Well, Tom, how are yo' gooin' on at the cottage?"

"All right, gaffer, on'y the o'd ooman's gooin' bald!"

"What did you say Tom?"

"The missis is gooin' bald."

"How's that, my good lad?"

"Well, it's a this'nin gaffer—the bedstid slopes so much her slips adown the bed, an' I pules her back by her yar, an' some comes off every time."

◇   ◇   ◇

Adam P. was a droll old butty, whose ways and conversation had quaint turns of their own. Shouting to his "whimsey" man he sometimes said:

"I say, surree lad, thee be'st a windin' the sun down, but thee bisna' windin' much coal up."

Meeting a number of men leaving the pits early he asked:

"Why binna yo' at work, lads?"

"We hanna got no pikes, gaffer."

Shaking his sides with laughter he said:

"Pikes! It hinna pikes yo' wantin', it's cups an' pints, it's cups an' pints, my lads."

He had his own way of offering inducements to return to work.

"If yo'll goo down again, I'll mak' the pikes work by themselves. I'll get a gimlet an' bore a hole, an' put a "tom-fly" in every helve, an' won't they buzz an' mak' the pikes do all the work themselves, while yo' just ho'din' them—that's all." Then the old wag would get down his gimlet, and after boring a hole in a "pike-helve," would hunt round for a "tom-fly." But of course the "tom-fly" was in the big bottle of ale he took care to send down the pit.

Many Bilston men served under Wellington in the "Twenty three years War," and when what remained of these returned after the victory at Waterloo, there were many and great rejoicings. In the middle of the space on Swan Bank, an ox was roasted whole. A great fire was made, and the carcase secured to a horizontal pole, which of course was worked by a handle. To turn this, in due course a collier—not long from Old Broseley—was set. The job seemed pleasant and full of promise. More than one envied him and said:

" Surree lad! let's tak' thee off a bit."

But Joe wouldn't share his privilege, and gruffly declined any help. Presently the fire burnt up, the crackling beef threw out great heat, and Joe moist with perspiration, and half blinded with smoke, wished for a respite. Looking at the man who offered to help he said laughingly:

" Aye, my good lad, thee might'st gi'e me a turn or two arter all."

In response the young collier threw off his jacket, and began some lusty turns of the handle. When Joe had mopped his grimy face he turned to see how the fellow was doing his work. To his horror he saw he was turning the carcase the opposite way. Instantly he brought the young fellow's services to an end by a tremendous blow in the face, shouting as he did so:

" That's the wrong way, thee be'st all unroastin' him."

◊   ◊   ◊

An old butty who had pits on the Willenhall Road was noted for his oddity. One Monday morning a man turned up at the pit who had been told not to come again. The butty looked at him and said:

" Thee be'st here, be'st, I reckon thee'st come to try thee tricks on me."

" Well conna I goo down an' work my notice out?"

" Thee shanna get a bit moor coal for me."

" Oh all right, we shan see," and with these words the man turned to go. But the butty had not done with him and shouted:

" I did'na tell thee to goo."

" But thee saidst I should'na goo down, gaffer."

" I did an' I'll be as good as my word, but thee shat'na ha' thee money for nothin', I'll find thee a job on the bonk an' if thee dus'na carry out my orders I'll send thee whum at a minute's notice."

"All right, I dunna care two straws."

The butty looked at him with a merry twinkle, and said: "Thee wait, dunna talk so fast. Fatch an armful o' straw out o' the stable an' bring it up the bonk to me, wut? The fellow carried it after him to the end of the bank, and the facetious old butty took up a single straw, and holding it in front of his mouth blew it into the air with a vigorous breath, and said:

"Theer! thee see'st that, thee'st got to tak' these straws one at a time, an' blow 'em down the bonk."

The man hesitated a moment, but he knew his master was a man of his word, and rather than lose his wages, settled to his humiliating task. Naturally he was the butt of joke and jibe from all that passed and after a few hours of ridicule was glad to get away on any terms.

◊   ◊   ◊

One of the most curious in the annals of the sporting life of the Black Country is recalled of an old cocker named Wilkes of Darlaston. His " duck-winged " champion was a very strong fighter, and was known far and wide. But on one occasion when encountering a Bilston bird, one of the cock's legs was badly broken. Loath to lose his favourite he dexterously amputated the injured limb and fondly nursed the poor thing until it had quite healed. Then he fitted on an artificial leg, to which he attached the usual steel spur, and the bird was able to strut about with something of its former pride. It is unnecessary to say that Wilkes' bird with the wooden leg drew countless spectators and inspired many a joke.

◊   ◊   ◊

THE GREEN BAIZE BAG

IN one of the Bilston works was found a musical enthusiast, who filled an important place in a Darlaston orchestra. The last rehearsal was fixed, but how to get away from his work was his problem. Like many another man in a similar trouble, he tried the familiar device of asking leave to attend a funeral; going to his manager, he said:

"Mr. T . . . . I want to get off this afternoon."

"Why, what's up?" asked the manager.

"My o'd grandmother's dead, an' I want to goo to the funeral."

"All right, off thee goo'st, but mind an' be here in the morning."

To his consternation when on his way to the rehearsal, with his double-bass in a green bag under his arm, Mr. T . . . drove past him in his master's gig, merely glancing, as he drove along. On the morning following, however, as he stood explaining his predicament to another workman, he saw the manager approaching them. "Look thee, he's comin', an' what the laws to say to him, I doh know!" he said excitedly.

When Mr. T . . . . drew near he said, while his eyes shone with grim humour, "Hadst got thee grandmother in that green baize bag yesterday?" Confounded and crestfallen he formed his mouth to speak, but Mr. T . . . . said: "Now doh thee say nuthin', the less thee say'st, the sooner thee't mend it; but doh thee do it again; thee cosn't bury thee grandmother twice, thee know'st."

GREETINGS

THERE was nothing quite like the passing nod of the miners. Those knowing, old-fashioned men put into a side bend of the neck and an accompanying grimace, great varieties of meaning that were quite unmistakeable. Just as whimsical, were their phrases of salutation. We have all heard the forms which mainly derive their drollness from the archaic modes of the dialect, such as:

"How do wut?"

"How is it o'd un'?"

"How be'st comin' up, my good lad?"

"How goos it, my little booty?"

The "little booty" was generally some burly butty, who turned the beam at sixteen stones, and whose face was a story of many good dinners.

"How binn'ee my love?" came often from the motherly old dames who bestowed their affectionate greetings upon all wholesome people who approached them.

The replies of the accosted will be recalled as frequently quaint and varied.

"Putty peart, thenk yo'!"

"Fit as a fightin' cock!"

"Amongst the middlen's!"

"Dooin' as well as they'n let me, my lad!"

"Nothin' to crack aboot!"

"I'm ommust winded, these o'd pipes bin welly done for!"

Sometimes we have heard them pass the "time o' day" with testy argument.

"Surree lad! I hanna see'd thee for times endways."

"I've see'd thee, them as wunna see, conna! I binna big enough I reckon."

"I'm allus glad to see a cliver chap loike thee."

"I tell thee I binna sure, I conna peay for a quart for thee loike some on 'em."

In the old days chummy miners rarely knocked others' doors, but frankly raised the latch and looked round the door with a cheery, "I'm a comin' in." Sometimes a more cere-monious person would rap, then a voice from within would ask: "Why dunno yo' come in?" or there would be the whimsical invitation: "Come in if yo'm fat."

The following was quite characteristic of these house-door greetings.

"I was just a-gooin' by, an' I thought I'd put my yed in an' see whether yo' wun alive or jed."

"We'm glad to clap eyes on thee, how's Ann Maria?"

"Oh, her's aboot again, her brought me another thousand a year, a fortneet comes Sunday.

"Yo' doh say soo! What is it, a lad or a child?"

"Oh as purty a wench as thee ever sidst."

"But that's dry bread!"

"I doh mind! t'others bin all lads."

"Well thee'st got some o' all soorts onnyhow now."

SEDGLEY STORIES

A CURIOUS CHRISTENING

THIS story carries us back to when the Rev. Mr. Lewis was Vicar of Sedgley.

One Saturday morning the maid answered a rap at the vicarage door to find two women there, one of them had in her arms a bundle which proved to contain a sick baby.

"We wantin' the vicar," said one.

"I'm afraid he can't see you, he doesn't see anyone on a Saturday morning," said the girl.

"But he'll ha' to see we, yoo goo an' tell him, he mun

come," urged the other woman. The maid hesitated, and the woman went on, " now you goo, an' say we'n come a'purpose, an' some'at bad's ommust sure to happen if he don't come," and as the maid went she called after her, " Now you hear— he mun come."

Mr. Lewis was not a hard and fast man, and so on this occasion he set aside his rule, and came to the door and asked:

" Well, my good women, what can I do for you?"

" Please, Mr. Lewis, we wantin' you to christen this 'ere child," one of them replied.

" Hadn't you better bring it to the church to-morrow?" he enquired.

" Oh, Mr. Lewis, it'll be jed by then," said the woman in a horror stricken voice.

" Well, if it's like that," said the minister, " you had better bring it into the vicarage," and they went into the house. " What's the name to be?" he asked.

" Oh, that don't matter, we leave it to you Mr. Lewis."

" Well, my name's William—suppose we call it William?"

Feeling greatly flattered, they replied: " That'll do very well, sir."

About a couple of hours later the maid was astonished to find them again at the door. " What do you want this time?" she enquired with some impatience.

" To see Mr. Lewis for sure," replied one of them. Rather curtly the girl said:

" I don't think he'll see you again this morning," which called forth the answer in an angry voice:

" By gommins he'll ha' to see we, he's med a nice mess on it for we."

" Why what's he done," queried the maid curiously.

" Never thee mind—thee fatch Mr. Lewis."

When the vicar came he enquired: " Well, what have you done?"

" It ain't what we'n done, it's what you'n done, Mr. Lewis."

" Come now, tell me what I've done!"

" You'n christened this 'ere child, William, an' her's a wench!'

The parson smiled, and said, " I'm sorry."

They felt some annoyance at his merry twinkle, and remarked with a tone of injury:

" It ain't no laughing matter, Mr. Lewis—wheer would her ha' gone to, if her'd ha' died wi' a lad's naame?"

THE LAWYER'S MATCH

MR. B., an old Black Country lawyer who was a rank old wag, found his match in a jolly mill-waggoner from Sedgley.

"Tom," said he one day, "they tell me mill-waggoners never go to Heaven, they are such a lot of rogues!"

"Wus than lawyers, bin they, Mr. B.?"

"Aye! everybody knows that!"

"Then they bin a bad lot for sure but onnyhow, I knowed a mill-waggoner who went to Heaven reet enough. When he got to the gates, Peter asked him 'what bin yo?' an' he answered 'a mill waggoner.' Peter turned rough an' replied 'this is no place for mill-waggoners, you'd better try the t'tother.' But just then there was a rush, an' a crush, an' he managed to squeeze in. When the gate was closed Peter noticed him, an' said, 'you are in, I see, but you had better get out again.'

The man, however, was stupid, an' said: 'I'm in, an' in I mean to stay.' 'Then,' said Peter, 'you'll have to be tried, an' I'll find a lawyer to defend you.' All night he searched Heaven through, but failed to find a lawyer."

The mill-waggoner laughed slyly at his own story, and Mr. B. said: "Go on with thee, I'll give thee best this time, Tom; thee cost tell a good story, anyhow."

COSELEY TALES

OLD AMOS

COSELEY tales have a quite characteristic flavour of their own.

This part of the Black Country has produced a rare crop of quaint characters, and amongst them, Amos the schoolmaster was one of the oddest. In his day any man whom some bodily defect incapacitated from manual work was considered suitable to teach the children of the working classes. Amos was an undergrown, droll, little figure, rendered more comical by his unsuitable and ill-fitting clothes.

His patrons, the then owners of the Cannon Foundry, kept him well supplied with left off garments of stylish cut, which always gave him too much room; and placed him at the mercy of idle jokers. When replying to his tormentors he was at a sorry disadvantage, a sort of "click clack" in his mouth, called forth further taunts, and in the school the boys were not slow to entertain one another with grimacing mimicry of their poor dominee.

A story illustrates his style of speech, and the quality of his influence. One day a woman came to see him ,and said:

"Amos, thee bis'na abringin' my lad on very well, I think."

With surprise he answered:

"Baint I?—I thought he was agettin' on all right."

But the woman persisted:

"I tell thee, he hai'nt acomin' on."

Amos thereupon called the lad to him, and said:

"Thee bisn'a learnin' nothin' thee mother says, but I'll show her that ha'int right. Now what's M-I-L-K spell?"

"I doh know," said the lad stupidly.

"Think," said Amos.

"I cor tell thee."

"Come, try."

Then Amos had an inspiration: "What's thee mother put in her tay?" he asked.

Instantly the lad's face brightened up and he said: "I know—rum!"

"Theer," said Amos triumphantly, "I told thee he's one o' my best lads!" but the woman had gone, the mention of her weakness was enough, and she did not stop to hear any comment from Amos.

BILSTON STORIES OF THE EARLY DAYS

A MERRY TRIO

In a hard winter, somewhere about the 1840s, a butcher, whose shop stood on the "flags" near the Balloon inn, had several pigs die with swine fever. Naturally he desired to keep his misfortune secret, and entrusted his son, then a lively youth, with the removal of the pigs. He, in turn took into his confidence the son of another shopkeeper and another youth, who saw great possibilities in the exploit.

Very late at night they removed the first pig, which they carried into Pinfold Street, near the "Big Coal" house, when hearing footsteps they dropped their load in fright, and hid themselves. Very soon some puddlers coming home from a short turn, fell over the obstruction. To them the pig was a windfall; they gladly bore it off, well-pleased with their luck, and had a rare feast.

The next night, number two was carried along Pinfold Street to a little pit, then working on land opposite to St. Luke's Church. The "bond" was down, and the "whimsy-man" asleep, or away from his post. Approaching quietly, the youths dropped the carcase down the pit shaft and then ran off.

They had conveyed the third pig as far as old lady W's., who lived near the Acorn inn, when a mischievous idea caught them. Seeing a glimmer of light, they peeped through the old lady's window, and saw sitting on one side of the fire-place the old lady's daughter, and on the other, the daughter's young man. The mother was just crossing the room with a candle in her hand, in preparation for retiring for the night. With cunning silence, the jokers reared the pig, frozen hard and stiff, against the house door.

A stone thrown at the door brought about the tragedy. The old lady, still holding the candle, innocently lifted the latch, when the log of pork fell forward into the room, laying her along the floor, and shaking the lighted candle from her hand. Startled and astounded by the gruesome intrusion, the young man rushed to the door breathing-out slaughter, but the tricksters were for the moment clear.

One of them, however, gave a clue. Having run down towards Market Street, he doubled back, and was walking carelessly past the scene of confusion when his courage failed, and he began to run. While chasing him they struck the trail of another. This one rushed up High Street, into Beebee's entry, and ran against an old woman, who had come out of a little house at the back.

"Hide me! Hide me! they are after me," he appealed and not in vain, for though she resented being tumbled against, she took him into the house, and shutting him in the coal hole, blew out her candle and sat down. Soon there was a rap, and the door opened, and someone who could not be seen, enquired:

"Anybody come in here?"

The pursuer found the old lady sitting alone in the glimmering firelight; yawning sleepily she asked:

"Aye, what dost want?"

"Has there e'er a chap come in here?"

"Aye, aye, what is it?" Then she settled her head for another doze. He tried again, but only got

"Aye, aye, what dost want?" which she shouted whilst she held her hand to her ear. Satisfied the lad was not there, he went on further. The fugitive then ran along the yard into the well-known passage at the back of the buildings, and placing his foot in a convenient hole in the wall, climbed into his father's yard and was soon safe in the house. His father who heard the hue and cry, came in and asked:

"Is our John in?"

"Oh yes," came a friendly voice. So John escaped, and the others too, we believe, and the mystery was not cleared up for long after.

SCOTT HYNDS

OUR story is associated with the Bell inn, an old hostelry of the eighteenth century. It will be recalled as an old fashioned house standing well back from the footpath, and marked by the swinging sign of a Bell. It was much frequented by miners, and was from early days a house of many sports. At the back there is still standing the old bull-stable, where the club kept its champion. Nearby was the bowling green, and also the marble alley, where players lingered while daylight lasted.

Our rather gruesome narrative carries us back well over a hundred years. The approach of the midnight hour found a group of men revelling at the Bell, when the conversation turned on the fate of a local criminal. Scott Hynds, the notorious highway murderer, had just been hanged, and his body placed in chains at the corner of Gibbet Lane. A boasting fellow was challenged to visit the gibbet, and ask Scott Hynds about his health when the church clock tolled the hour of twelve. The wager arranged, the adventurer started. Before he got to the end of the lane he could hear the weird grind and clink of the chains, as the body swung to the push of the restless night wind. But he worked up his courage and saw the matter through. Going right up to the Gibbet, he enquired:

"Scott Hynds! how be'st tonight?" when to his amazement a quavering unearthly voice answered:

"I'm very cold and weary—get me a warm drink!"

Waiting for no more, shivering and frightened out of his

wits, he ran back breathless to the Bell. The wagerers showed scepticism:

" Thee has'na bin—thee has'na had time," was the general challenge.

Then he told his strange story, to the uproarious merriment of the fellows, and just as he finished, another man whom he had not missed entered the room when the laughter redoubled. This man was the ghost who had answered for Scott Hynds, it being part of the plot for him to get to the Gibbet first, and, if possible, scare the other man.

" THEE BE'EST DITTO "

NANNY was a thrifty old body who had her little home amongst the miners' families in the Workhouse Fold. Day by day she took her little book to Mr. I—— the grocer, who entered line after line, and when the meagre debt had grown for a week, she honestly wiped it off.

One day her husband, Jack the sinker, coming home in a bad mood said:

" Nan, thee bisna dooin' reet wi' o'd I—— the grocer."

"What's mean Jack?" asked Nan in pained surprise, " Theed'st better mind what thee be'st sayin' my lad."

" I know what I bin a sayin' my wench, he looked crossways at me as I com'd by, an' I con tell thee bisna payin' off thee score every wick."

Nanny indignantly retorted:

" Thee be'st a liar, Jack, I allus pays it off."

" I tell thee, thee dusn't; I woipes my score off every wick, an' thee ought'st to do the same—I shanna be able to face the mon!"

" I tell thee I do, an' I'll show thee some'at as cor tell no lies."

In the meantime she had reached her little shop-book and placed it in front of him saying:

" If thee wut'na believe me, look at that."

Jack looked at it, puzzled a minute over it, and then said: " I know'd theer was some'at wrong—what's that?" pointing to a line in the book, " an' that, an' that?"

" Nothin'! It's thee as is boff-homblin'," said Nan.

" Well look for thee self," he replied sharply. She looked at it after wiping her glasses, but had to confess:

" I conna say, I binna no scholar, as thee know'st." At which Jack started on a new line.

"I cor mak' it out, is o'd I——a dooin' thee down, dost think? Thee'st never had them things sure enough."

Not knowing what else to say, Nan answered:

"I'll goo an' ax Mr. I——;" and slipping her shawl over her head she disappeared down the Fold. Reaching the shop she attacked Mr. I—— with:

"Look here Mr. I.——! what's this, an' this? I hanna had these things," pointing to several lines in the book.

The grocer took the book from her, and looking at it remarked with a smile:

"Oh, I see what's the matter, that's my son for you, he's got these new fangled ways."

Then showing it to Nanny, he went on to say:

"You had half pound of bacon on Monday, didn't you?"

"I did, Sir."

"And another on Tuesday?"

"You'm reet, Sir."

"And again on Wednesday and Thursday?"

"That's quite reet."

"Well, that's all it means, but my son has put 'ditto, ditto,' instead of writing it all over again. 'Ditto' means the same again you know."

"Well, I bin an o'd fule," she exclaimed, "thank you Mr. I——I know'd it were all reet."

When she returned, Jack asked:

"Well, Nan, what dost mak' on it?"

With an indignant outburst, Nan replied:

"I'll tell thee what I mak' on it, I mak' out as I'm an o'd fule, an' thee bist 'Ditto'."

THE WIT OF BILSTON JACK

MR. A. was a prosperous tradesman, and well known the town over. To a well-groomed presence, he added the taste of an ardent sportsman. In his day he was rarely absent from the hunt, when his beautiful steed, and prize hounds were much admired.

One day when returning from the hunt, he met a party of poor fellows under the care of a keeper from Burntwood Asylum. One of the patients, known as Bilston Jack, recognising Mr. A. called out:

"Hallo Mr. A., wheer have you been?"

The keeper was shocked, and turning to Jack said:

"Hush, hush—you must not speak to people in the road."

60

To Mr. A. he said:

"I hope you won't mind him, sir."

Mr. A. was a sensible man with a kind heart; smiling he replied:

"Oh it's all right—he's an old friend of mine!"

Taking heart, poor Jack left the ranks, and approached Mr. A., repeating his question, he enquired:

"Wheer have you been, sir?"

"I have been hunting, Jack," he replied.

Stroking the horse, Jack remarked with admiration:

"This is a nice horse, Mr. A!"

"You are right, Jack, everyone says the same."

"How much is he wuth, Mr. A.—if I may be so bold?"

"A hundred pounds at least."

"An' these bin nice hounds as well!"

"They are, Jack."

"How much bin they wuth, Mr. A?"

"I have just won a prize of ten pounds with them—they are worth that at the very lowest, Jack."

"What do you do with them, sir?"

"Oh I hunt with them, of course."

"What do you hunt, Mr. A?"

"The fox."

"The fox, I've never sin a fox. What do you hunt the fox for, sir?"

"For its brush of course."

"What's that?"

"Its tail."

"How much is that wuth, sir?"

"I don't know, Jack—half-a-crown perhaps."

"Half-a-crown! then you'd better be gooin' sir, or they'll be puttin' you in theer," said Jack, pointing to the asylum.

"Why Jack?" asked Mr. A. in surprise.

"For sending one hundred and ten pounds after half-a-crown," said poor Jack.

◇   ◇   ◇

A BIT O' MOONSHINE

EARLY in the last century an odd character, who lived alone at Woodsetton, used to tell a joke against himself. There were few abstainers in those times, and the old man drank himself merry most days, and returned to his lonely cottage with his brain far from clear. One cold moon-light night he turned in as usual, hoping for " a drap o' hot tae " before going to bed. He had left the time-honoured raker on the fire, but for some reason it had gone out; all seemed cold and black when he entered and closed the door behind him, and he muttered: " it's all up wi'e my drap o' tae, I see." But when he moved he saw a little wavering bright speck amongst the coals; reaching the "ballies" he sat down to blow it into a·flame, but when he sat down he could not see it—the light had gone. Calling himself several picturesque names he rose, and grumpishly threw the blow-bellows into a corner of his little kitchen. But when he turned round again, curiously enough there was surely a bright lively spot in the middle of the grate. When he had recovered the bellows and sat down to blow, it could not be seen. Then his muddled brain began to clear a bit; he noticed that when he moved back again it vanished. Where was the key to the mystery, why didn't the fire "tinder up" when he "blowed it?" Then he saw through it all—on turning round he espied a slender thread of brilliant moon-light, piercing the darkness through a pin-hole in the shutter. He had been trying the power of his "ballies" on a bit o' moonshine.

MORE HUMOUR OF THE OLD BLACK COUNTRY

THE BUTTY, THE BAILEE AND THE DOGGY

A Londoner, who spent a week amongst the miners, in order to learn what he could concerning their conditions of life and work, employed a young collier as his guide. When they had been together a few days, he said to his guide:

"Look here, my man, you have talked a lot about the 'Butty,' and the 'Ground Bailee,' and the 'Doggy,' will you tell me the difference between them, and what they do?"

"Well," replied the collier, " it's a this'nin, sir. The Ground Bailee's the mon what cusses the Butty; the Butty's the mon what cusses the Doggy; an' the Doggy's the mon what cusses the colliers. Now do' yo' see, sir?"

PICTURESQUE DIRECTIONS

THE period was over a hundred years ago; the place Catherine's Cross, Darlaston. A stranger asked a native:
"Can you tell me the way through Bilston to Woodsetton?"
"I con, I allus goo anunst the Duckin' Pule, an' on to the Fiery Holes, by Hangman's Row, then past Gibbet Lane, on to Hell Lane, an' along theer to Ketchem's Corner, then on to Sodom. When thee get'st theer, theed'st better ax agen."
"Don't I goo o'er the Gallows Bridge, an' by Bug Holes?"
"No. them plasen bin out o' thee way miles endways."

GRACE BEFORE MEAT

BLACK country funerals have often been occasions of great feasting. Very often an invitation was couched as one to come and have a bit of enjoyment.

Some years ago, a number of working men were gathered in a small house, after laying the remains of their late friend in the cemetery. The table was bountifully spread with good things, and the host invited them to take their places, and set to. When they were seated and about to begin, one of them said:

"Wait a bit lads! Dunna let us forget Him as sends the 'fittals,' let's ax a blessing?"

"Well, thee ax it, theeself," replied one, when he said the following unusual grace:

"Oh Lord! gi'e we strength to ate all as is put afore we. One word's as good as ten, for Christ's sake. Amen."

There was a flavour of oddity about the circumstances, but nothing irreverent.

THE COAL'S COME

MANY years ago in the Lunt, at Bilston, there were many small cottages set in the midst of the gardens. In one of these lived Ned—, a well-known collier and heavy drinker. Ned gave his wife little enough for house-keeping, and generally pawned his "lowance-coal" to the publican. Many a time he promised his wife that the next load should come home, but he so repeatedly broke his word, that her disappointment gave place to disgust.

One stormy night, after words about the missing coal, the wind blew the chimney down on to the roof; the terrible noise woke up Ned, when he asked his wife what was the matter? In her scorn, she answered:

"Thee'dst better get up! the coal's come at last."

A QUAINT FUNERAL STORY

A Black Country woman, rather noted for her nagging ways, was in other respects said to be a decent sort. After many years of married life, during which her husband suffered martyrdom from her tireless tongue; she was taken ill, became a great sufferer, and in the end died. Notwithstanding her serious fault, her husband had great regard for her, and resolved to give her a respectable funeral. In those days it was reckoned a great honour to be carried shoulder-high to the grave, and her husband arranged to give her this coveted distinction.

On the way to the church-yard, the bearers had to pass a sharp corner, and in doing so one of them took a false step, and the coffin coming into collision with the wall, fell to the ground. The shock sprung off the lid, and to their horror the body moved. A doctor coming on the scene pronounced the woman to be still living, and ordered her to be taken home. With careful nursing she fully recovered, and for some time happily kept her tongue under control.

Alas, after the terror had been forgotten, the old habit returned, and her good man's trouble recurred. Once again however, she was taken ill, and this time really died. Again her husband determined to do things well, and have her carried "shoulder high." He wanted to be quite certain, however, this time, and so he said to the bearers:

"Mind that corner this time, lads!"